The Mini Book of Teaching Tips for Librarians

2nd Edition

Andrew Walsh

The moral right of Andrew Walsh to be identified as the author of this work has been asserted in accordance with the Copyright, Designs and Patents act of 1988.

Published by Innovative Libraries, 2018.
Sepapaja tn 6
Lasnamäe linnaosa,
Tallinn, Harju maakond
15551
Estonia

UK contact address:
195 Wakefield Road, Lepton, Huddersfield. HD8 0BL.
andywalsh@innovativelibraries.org.uk
http://innovativelibraries.org.uk/
@PlayBrarian

"The Burgess sisters arrived together. Tara and Lainie do a little bit of everything. Sometimes dancers, sometimes actresses. Once they were librarians, but that is a subject they will only discuss if heavily intoxicated."

Erin Morgenstern, The Night Circus

May we all do a little bit of everything… and enjoy talking about it after a drop too much drink.

Contents

Introduction

Welcome to this mini book! When I started this, I had in mind a set of Tarot sized cards with about 50(ish) cards of teaching tips for librarians – a mix of general tips and actual interventions that could be dropped into a teaching session.

I thought people could dip into the deck, or perhaps pull their favourite few to the front to refer to again.

After writing a (rather expensive) book in the past of Active Learning ideas for librarians, I was concerned that these cards should not only be easy to dip into and pull out your favourites, but as affordable as possible too!

Unfortunately at the sort of volumes I was expecting to sell, large playing cards seemed more expensive than I'd like to pass onto you, the reader.

Hence this little book! The pages are roughly the same size as the cards would have been, but cost a fraction of the amount to print.

I hope that explains the layout. In the first edition I pretty much kept to the restrictions of one small page per tip (with very few exceptions) and resisted the urge to waffle and expand unnecessarily.

After feedback, I've relaxed this slightly for some of the "ideas" pages (see below!) to make things a little clearer in the second edition.

I hope this is a nice balance between the single page tips in the first half and the teaching ideas later on. This second edition is also slightly extended compared to the first edition, with a few more teaching ideas and significantly more of the teaching tips.

I've also added some further reading towards the end of the book, focussing on practical books for teaching ideas.

So dip into the following pages to find roughly half the pages containing general tips and definitions, and half the pages giving brief descriptions of ideas you could use in your own teaching. Some are old favourites, some you might not have seen before, but hopefully all useful to some of you...

The following pages are general teaching "tips" and ideas that can help to inform and improve your teaching.

Active Learning

I tend to take an Active Learning approach to as much of my teaching as possible and would strongly recommend others do to. It suits the skills we should be trying to help our learners develop.

A quick and dirty definition of it is simply "learning by doing". So don't tell people about things. Don't give them masses of facts and expect them to remember. Get them to carry out tasks themselves, as this approach allows them to build upon their existing knowledge and learn new things (and their relevance). The examples of teaching interventions in this mini book can be seen as active learning examples.

It is a *Constructivist* approach to teaching and learning.

All the things

Lots of librarians (myself included) see many of our learners for one teaching session (one-shots) and never again…

So it is really tempting to try to tell them *all the things*. To fit as much in as possible during that session so we know we've covered everything (we think) important.

This never works. Our learners get overwhelmed with information. We lose all interactivity as this quickest way to pass large volumes of information to a class is to talk at them. They retain very little of that information we think is vital!

Instead, take a step back, cover less information in a more interactive way. Focus on enabling them to learn for themselves – they will seek out the other things if they need them!

Assessment Types

A very brief guide to different assessment types!

Formative assessment is checking what students know / have learnt so you can tweak your teaching or give them feedback and enable deeper learning.

Diagnostic assessment is similar, but often aims at checking knowledge at the start.

Summative assessment comes at the end of a chunk of learning (course, module, etc.) and allows them to show what they have learnt (often counts towards a qualification).

Ipsative assessment is where students self-report how much they know and is normally used to compare knowledge at the start and end of a session.

Attention Span

People have shorter attention spans than you might assume! They tend to be much shorter than a typical 50 minute class.

When planning your teaching, aim to split down any session into (roughly) 10 minute sections, with each section focussing on a different type of activity.

10 minutes should be short enough to make sure people can concentrate properly on each section, with the change in activity acting like a <reset> on their ability to pay attention and stay focussed.

Backward Design

I thought this might be worth mentioning, as often people focus on activities and forget about what they want people to learn!

Backward design is a way of planning your teaching that stresses the importance of the desired learning outcomes of a teaching session.

You then decide what activities match those desired outcomes and you *only* include those activities.

It is nicely summarised on the Learning-theories.com[1] as 3 steps (in order!):

1. Identify Desired Outcomes
2. Identify Acceptable Evidence
3. Plan Learning Experiences and Instruction

---

[1] https://www.learning-theories.com/backward-design.html.

Behaviourism

Behaviourism is a learning theory that puts the teacher firmly in charge. If this is how you believe people learn most effectively, then you are likely to focus on predefined goals and outcomes, often around the learning of "facts", rather than problem solving.

This is often the predominate theory that drives didactic lecturing, regular (often multiple choice) tests, and learning facts by rote.

It treats the learner like a clean slate ready to be filled with knowledge and their behaviour shaped by positive and negative stimuli, so regular testing is needed to measure progress and reward or punish accordingly.

Bloom's Taxonomy

This is one of those things that is often talked about when discussing learning & teaching. The bit of it most likely to be useful is the "Cognitive Domain", which assigns names (the taxonomy) to different levels of understanding and learning.

Slightly changed from the 1950s original, the revised levels are Remembering, Understanding, Applying, Analysing, Evaluating, Creating. Search online and you'll find lots of images of pyramids showing this!

Essentially, it's thought that the higher up the pyramid (towards "Creating"), the "better" or deeper the learning! So when setting learning objectives, remember you should be trying to move your learners from "remembering" things to "creating" new knowledge.

Blended Learning

Rather than purely online, or just face to face, blended learning is simply a mixture of the two.

It mixes online materials, which have a strong element of student control in when and where they access them, as well as how long they spend on them, with regular face to face meetings.

So the face to face sessions will often be used to consolidate learning from the online materials and may be relatively infrequent.

Blended learning has no generally agreed definition, but normally has a significant proportion of time spent online compared to face to face. It could be seen as similar to the flipped classroom approach, but heavier on the online time.

Constructivism

Constructivism puts the learner at the centre of the learning process, rather than the teacher.

It recognises that everyone starts with prior knowledge and experiences and must build upon that to develop new knowledge – the opposite to the (more traditional) behaviourist approach.

It states that we can't be given new knowledge, but instead we always try to integrate new facts into our existing knowledge – this subjective representation is always unique to ourselves. Constructivism says learning always takes place in this way, so it makes sense to teach in ways that recognise it. As such, pedagogical approaches that recognise this way of learning will tend to give opportunities for problem solving, group work, and discussion.

Differentiation

Differentiation can mean one of 2 things!

1) Making sure that your lesson has variety in it so that people do a different range of activities (may be used in relation to learning styles)

2) Being aware that learners in any group will come with a range of prior knowledge and abilities, so making sure that the activities you provide can stretch all learners. If you plan well, you should aim for no-one being frustrated as they can't keep up, and no-one bored because they haven't been sufficiently stretched (or occupied).

Try to build differentiation into your lesson plan when planning the learning objectives and activities.

Differing viewpoints

Try to consider different viewpoints in your teaching. The materials you or your learners are using may have been written from one viewpoint, your background may bring in biases and opinions of their own, and both of these may be alien to some or all of your learners.

If the content is to be meaningful to your learners, and they are to critically engage with it, then you must address these implicit biases in your teaching.

Is your teaching and your materials coming from a male dominated, white, straight cisgendered, Western point of view?

Try to enrich your teaching by bringing in differing viewpoints.

Embodied Cognition

This refers to the idea that we don't just think with our heads or brains, some of the information processing and problem solving takes place through our bodies too.

Giving people an opportunity to think with their bodies, or just with their hands, can result in different results within a class.

Any learning that involves model building takes advantage of this, and it is at the foundation of the Lego™ Serious Play™ methodology.

Even without using it directly, you can take advantage of this by leaving materials on the table for your learners to mould (modelling clay), build with (blocks, Lego™, etc.), or doodle with.

Flipped Classroom

This is an old idea, revived in recent years as something "new" with the increase in blended learning.

In a nutshell, "flipping" the classroom encourages us to use the face to face time we have with students to facilitate discussion, work on problem solving and projects, or other things that add more value than the transmission of "facts".

In a flipped classroom environment, we will normally set work the learners are expected to do in advance. This may be to watch videos, do online tutorials, or read some materials.

When we meet the students we can then build on the things they've learnt by themselves and help them apply and deepen their knowledge.

Large Groups

Large group teaching is different. Unless you realise why, the difference between teaching small and large groups can be confusing and hard to deal with.

Simply put, the larger a group gets, the more people act like herd animals. We are scared of appearing different, or standing out. Attempts at interactivity or discussion can often fail. They daren't do anything that makes them stand out!

So to bring interactivity or discussion into large group teaching you must let them hide or show them that they are safe. Use polls with phone or voting pads. Split them into small groups. Encourage group play across the room and throughout the session. But most of all recognise that anything you do that means people stand out from the crowd will be problematic!

Learning Styles

You may hear learning styles being talked about. This refers to the idea that all students learn differently and that everyone has a preferred style of learning.

Most common is the VAK or VARK model, describing Visual (particularly images), Aural (listening, voice and music), Read/Write (the written word), and Kinaesthetic (movement, thinking with hands).

The idea that people have a preferred way of learning **isn't** supported by the evidence, so don't take it literally. However, it can sometimes be a convenient shortcut when planning, to make sure you are providing a range of activities to help with attention spans that will be shorter than your session!

Lecturing

The approach I take to teaching involves a minimal amount of "lecturing". I tend not to spend extended periods of time talking at students.

Even with large quantities of students I try to bring some interactivity into my teaching and try to break up a session into shorter chunks of content if possible.

That said, sometimes a lecture suits the content. Sometimes it suits the presenter, and a great lecture can be engaging, informative, and enjoyable.

So if *you* are a good performer and are able to use lecture style teaching effectively, then there is nothing wrong with this style of teaching.

For most of us though, it's easier to learn how to be an effective facilitator and workshop style leader, rather than a great lecturer.

Lesson plans

Always try to prepare a lesson plan.

It helps you to ensure that you are planning content that matches your aims and objectives. It can prompt you to split the lesson into manageable chunks (**see attention spans**). It can help you check if you are assessing the learning that should be taking place. It can keep you on track during the lesson itself, act as a reminder of what you need to prepare beforehand (and take with you!), and provide a place to write down quick reflections during / after the session. Last, but not least, it can be an aide memoire the next time you plan a similar session, or a guide to follow if someone else needs to take your class.

Learning objectives

Make sure you write aims and proper learning objectives for any session you lead. The aim is a general overview of what the session is about. The learning objectives are more detailed and should be measureable targets that your learners can show they have learnt by the end of the session.

One way of thinking about learning objectives is making them SMART (Specific, Measurable, Attainable, Relevant, and Time Focussed).

Preferably differentiate using the objectives too – so have learning objectives that *everyone* should be able to do, some trickier ones that *most* will, and some stretch goals that *very few* will achieve.

Learning while walking

Consider taking your learners out of the classroom. It provides a change of scene and so helps to disrupt their expectations of how the class will work.

It also has the benefit of increasing blood flow to the brain, and if you send them somewhere "green", can be shown as having a positive effect on mood.

At its simplest, you can just send them to a fixed point (and back!) in small groups as a way of timing group discussions.

If you fancy something more complicated, there is a whole field called psychogeography which experiments in changing how we think about the landscape around us. Many people have used these ideas in their teaching and learning.

Mini Librarians

It is not your job to turn your learners into mini-librarians (unless you are a lecturer on a librarianship type course!).

Whatever sector you work in, you are there to help them develop their skills and knowledge to do their jobs, their studies, or their academic research more effectively.

This doesn't mean they have to approach searching for and using information like the "ideal" might suggest, or even do it in the way you would.

Instead focus on giving them the knowledge and skills to work effectively *in their own context.* Facilitate their learning, don't try to dictate exactly how they should approach things.

Mixing up groups

Often when a group of people come into your teaching space they sit down next to the same people as in any other session. They tend to stick closest to the people they know well already.

As a teacher it can be beneficial to mix the groupings up, to generate new dynamics, and new ideas.

There are lots of ways of doing this randomly. Try one of these two:

- Number people as they come into the room (1 to x, where x is the number of groups you want). Then tell people to move so all the same numbers are together.
- Find some sweets with enough colours to match the number of groups you need. Give everyone a sweet as they enter the room and then tell them to form groups based on sweet colour.

New teaching ideas

People have been teaching each other new things since the dawn of time. Ways of teaching and learning come in and out of fashion, technology often influencing this (think of the printing press!), but there are rarely any new or spectacularly different teaching ideas to be had.

So don't try and think of new things! Instead read widely, pay attention to how people learn, watch other people teach, and *apply that to your context.*

What makes things feel innovative or new is simply how you apply them and the context they are applied in, not whether anyone else has done something similar before! So take ideas from as many sources as possible and think how you will apply them to improve your teaching.

Object based learning

Object based learning is a teaching approach based around learning through focussing on objects that are normally provided by the instructor.

It is closely related to active learning and experiential learning and is a social constructivist approach.

Particularly popular in museums, this might suit special collections and archives as an approach.

Learners are normally given an object and asked to make observations about it, including drawing meaning from it, make comparisons to other objects, or discuss its function.

As such, if you work in an institution that uses object based learning, these sessions are ideal team teaching opportunities with subject specialists.

Pedagogy

Pedagogy is what should inform your teaching. It is the discipline that connects the theory of learning to your own practice.

If you can consider your own pedagogical approach, it will make you a more effective teacher. You should draw from learning theories, the needs of your learners, and the subject matters you deal with. Combine these with your own strengths and weaknesses as a teacher to evolve a pedagogical approach that suits you and your learners.

Despite what many books will try to tell you, there is no one "correct" approach that you should take. Instead there will be approaches that happen to be particularly suited to both you and your students – you must decide on the effectiveness of these yourself.

Permission to Play

When our learners come into a teaching space they are conditioned by long experience to act in a particular way.

Especially in lecture theatre type settings, they will expect to sit and listen to an "expert" at the front. They will not expect to think deeply for themselves, to carry out activities, or contribute significantly to the learning of the whole group.

The expectations can also depend on the "normal" teaching in their subject area.

If you want to use activities that contrast with these prior expectations, you have to give them permission (explicitly, and implicitly) to break this conditioning.

Consider layout, warm up exercises at the beginning, and anything else that clearly signals that it is not a "normal" classroom. This will help to give them permission to play in your session.

Plan for additional needs

Try to make sure your teaching is as inclusive as possible, addressing the needs of all learners.

So if possible, check in advance if any of them have any additional learning needs and consider these while planning the session.

It is much simpler to plan for needs in advance than trying to react to them once a session has started. It will also be a much better and less stressful experience for you and the learners.

Playful Learning

Playful learning uses games, creative techniques, and playful approaches, in order to enable the benefits of play to come into learning.

When people play they are often referred to as stepping into a magic circle of play, where the rules of the normal world no longer apply.

This playful environment is seen as a safe place to experiment and fail without real world consequences. It means that people can express ideas freely, it helps learners see things from alternative perspectives, and it allows the practice of skills, all in that safe environment. Play is also fun, naturally engaging, and helps people remember content more effectively.

Playful learning fits into the idea of social constructivism, along with many of the other examples in this short book.

Polling software

This is particularly good for bringing a little bit of interactivity into a large group session. Polling software replaces "clickers" that were popular a few years ago, and instead uses students own devices.

Most work across multiple platforms and often allow responses by text message or (mobile friendly) webpages, allowing people to respond from phones, tablets, or fixed computers.

Most have free versions, plus paid for versions with extra functionality. Try Kahoot (quite limited, but works great on phones), Polleverywhere (lots of options, but larger groups need a paid for licence), Mentimeter (lots of options & free for larger groups), or Plickers (a different way of using it, students hold up cards to vote and the teacher uses their phone to automatically count votes!).

Preparation

Preparation and planning prevent poor performance (the "P" rule!). But make sure you carry out the *best* sort of preparation!

Complete a lesson plan and prepare any materials you need well in advance, don't leave it to the last minute.

But don't plan every tiny bit of the lesson down to the last detail, you need flexibility to react to unexpected circumstances. Instead, make sure your activities and content are well planned and flexible enough to give space for the unexpected. For example, well planned group discussion and activities can often be shortened and lengthened to ensure a session takes the correct amount of time.

Problem Based Learning

Worth mentioning as this can be a great approach to teaching information skills!

It allows the learners to set the skills you want them to learn in the context of a relevant problem and is a very student centred (rather than teacher centred) approach. It suits collaboration between information and subject specialists.

In this approach, you set a fairly open ended problem for them to complete, and through investigating it they learn skills and subject knowledge.

The instructor's job is to carefully scaffold them through the process, so they have enough support to start off, becoming more independent as they move towards a conclusion.

Reflection

To become a better teacher or trainer, you must be willing to constantly improve yourself. Reflection is a major way of doing this.

Immediately after a session, look at what happened. What went well? What could be improved? What will you stop doing?!

Consider leaving a space on your **lesson plan** for this, so you can jot down some notes immediately afterwards.

But also revisit those notes and consider a written reflective journal, a blog (it can be private!), or a vlog (video log) when you have more time.

Next time you teach a similar lesson, go back to these reflective notes again.

Rhizomatic Learning

A rhizome might be familiar to those of you who are gardeners – it's a plant that sends shoots out underground which pop up as new plants from new places as it spreads (think couch grass!).

Rhizomatic learning[2] says that learning happens best when we follow the paths that open up as we learn, rather than aim purely for pre-existing objectives. It puts the focus on groups or networks of learners and their environment, rather than the instructor and recognizes that all learning is interconnected.

It is a powerful idea in teaching as it recognises the agency of the learner as being even more important than the teacher.

---

[2] A nice summary & links from Dave Cormier http://davecormier.com/edblog/2011/11/05/rhizomatic-learning-why-learn/

Room Layout

Don't be afraid to change a room layout if you are able to.

The way a room is laid out influences your learners' expectations of how they should behave, together with what sort of learning will be taking place.

Straight rows of seats immediately set up the expectation that they will be passively listening to whoever is at the front of the room.

Seats all around tables, imply that they will be working in groups more than listening to an expert.

No seats or tables at all (or leaving the classroom) implies an active session where they will be expected to take a full part right from the beginning.

Try to make sure your room layout matches the sort of session you intend to run.

Scaffolding

Unless you use a very didactic style (stand at the front and talk at them!), scaffolding is an important idea to understand.

It refers to the idea that you structure a class (or series of classes) so that they get a lot of support when learning new ideas or skills. Your scaffold starts quite restrictive, with little movement available from the structure you've planned. As they progress, you can remove elements of the scaffold allowing more freedom as they gain understanding.

E.g. you might have a worksheet that lists the steps they take (with examples) in detail at the start. By the end of the session, you may be setting them a similar task without the steps (and examples) in detail for them to follow.

Setting expectations

At the start of every class try to make sure you set expectations effectively.

Make sure the room (and layout) is as suitable as possible, including removing unwanted distractions. Turn up on time (or early) preferably before your learners arrive and if you don't know the group, introduce yourself at the start.

Make sure your learners know the aim of the session and why this is relevant. Link this to prior learning if possible. Consider sharing your learning objectives too.

In short, make sure that when the learners arrive, everything is as ready for them as it can be and they know why they (and you) are there.

Slides

There is something about presentation software and slides that people struggle to resist – whether using PowerPoint, Prezi, or whatever!

They are a safety net to hide behind as a presenter and often they aren't necessary.

If you use slides, my top 5 tips are:

- Keep the amount of text low and fonts large, they should be easy to read at a glance. Use visuals instead.
- Don't read out your slides! Either say it or write it down – no need to do both.
- You can have more detailed slides (including your notes) that you make available afterwards.
- Using alternatives to PowerPoint does *not* make your slide deck better – you can have bad slides in any software package!
- Make PowerPoint non-linear by linking slides with (internal) hyperlinks.

Teaching Qualifications

There are many levels of teaching qualifications available. (Note: UK qualifications)

A teaching qualification doesn't just give you a piece of paper to show future or existing employers, it is a chance to reflect on your current practice and become a reflective, continually improving, practitioner.

A basic award that can be found at many FE colleges is the Level 3 award in teaching and learning. This is sometimes the basic level required to teach in FE.

The next level up is a Cert Ed. It brings in more theory and again can be found in FE colleges and some universities.

Often the Cert Ed can be continued and becomes the next level, PGCE. This is the normal Post Graduate level to take after a first degree.

TeachMeets

TeachMeets are informal meetings, normally free to attend, and often outside of standard working hours.

They are a great way of getting tips and ideas to improve your teaching, as well as an opportunity to share your own practice.

Typically, most people who attend are expected to briefly present something about their own practice. This may be a 5 or 10 minute talk, within a supportive environment. Other networking activities may take around the presentations as well.

TeachMeets[3] are easy to organise, so if you can't find one near you, don't be afraid of organising your own.

---

[3] For tips on organising them and lists of events - http://libteachmeet.pbworks.com

This is the end of the general "tips"! The following pages are ideas that could be dropped directly into your own teaching.

Assessment - Stand up, sit down

Ask the whole class to stand up.

Ask the class a question with two possible answers, preferably with as YES / NO or TRUE / FALSE answer. Tell them to stay standing for one response and to sit for the other.

Ask another question, but only those who got the first one correct take part.

Continue for as long as you want or need!

Assessment – What do you know?

Give a small (A5 or A6) piece of card for each student.

Ask them to write down how much they know about a topic, how long they spend carrying out a task, or how confident they feel carrying out a task.

Collect the responses together at the front of the class and collate them in a way you can easily read or display to the class.

At the end of a session ask the same question again and once more collate the responses – you may have to do this verbally or as a show of hands to save time collating the responses.

Compare the responses at the start & end of the session.

Assessment – Bag of fears

Use this to check what students are aware that they don't know and check for student reported improvement.

Distribute a small card to each student.

Ask them to write down the biggest fear about the topic you are about to cover.

Collect the responses at the front.

During an exercise in a session where you have a few minutes of time, scan through them and group according to "fears" expressed.

At the end of a session review each "fear" and ask if it has been addressed.

Assessment – True & False

Post signs around the room. They can be as few as two (so TRUE or FALSE can be used) or as many as you like that will fit in the room. These signs can indicate a range of preferences such as: Topics of interest; Questions about content; Possible solutions to a problem; Personal values; Quotations relevant to the subject.

Ask participants to go to the sign that most accurately reflects their preference.

Each group of people at a sign forms a group and spends 5 minutes amongst themselves discussing why they chose that one and feedback to the whole class.

Make sure there is enough space in the room for people to move safely from where they are sat to the prepared signs.

Assessment - I felt my way to a better search...

Prepare a large set of felt shapes – cut into flower and plant shapes (either readymade or homemade!), together with green coloured felt boards for them to stick to.

The important factor is not the models, but forcing the learners to reflect on their current knowledge and to explain that to someone else. The models are just a tool to allow that reflection, so don't allow too long or they will become more focussed on creating the object than reflecting on their knowledge and experience.

If a large group, split into smaller groups of two or three and give a felt board and an assortment of shapes to each group. If a smaller class, give a board to each person.

Give the class 2 or 3 minutes to create a felt garden representing their last search for information using your library's resources.

Ask them to briefly explain their models to the whole class.

If any common themes emerge that you weren't expecting, adapt your session to take this into account.

Although the example of searching for information is given here, it can be used to reflect upon any activity or state of knowledge you wish.

Note - This is adapted from a workshop presentation given by Bosch & Duong from California State University at LILAC in 2011.

Assessment – Poster tours

At the end of a group exercise, ask your learners to express their thoughts or findings on a piece of flip-chart paper. Each group then puts their sheet of paper on the wall of the room.

On your prompt, each group moves to the next group's poster and they spend a short period of time looking at it and discussing it amongst themselves. They then write down their comments directly on the poster in a different coloured pen.

Give each group a short amount of time (perhaps 1 or 2 minutes, depending on the time available overall) then signal the groups to move around the room

Repeat this until each group is back at their own poster.

The groups can then read comments the other groups have left for them.

Assessment – One minute paper

A simple, widely used, assessment idea. At the end of an exercise, or the end of the class, give the learners one minute to write the answer to a question you pose.

This could be anything you feel will make them reflect on the material that has just been covered.

Examples might be: "Summarise what you have learnt in this session"; "What is the key idea you have taken from this session"; or "What did you disagree with out of the material we covered today".

They can then pass them to you to check over. If you're doing this during the session (rather than at the end), try to build in an exercise afterwards they will need minimal support on so you have time to scan through them.

Feedback – By plane

A variation on the standard way of filling in a feedback sheet and dropping it off at the front on the way out! Just a bit of fun, but can also increase the number of people filling it in. Works well in a tiered lecture theatre.

Have a feedback sheet with whatever questions you want to ask on one side, plus instructions on how to fold a paper plane on the other.

At the end of the session hand out your feedback sheets and tell them that once they have filled it in, they should turn it into a paper plane and throw it to you.

If you want, you could have a box or other container at the front and give (small) prizes for anyone who gets their plane inside it!

Feedback – Stop, Start, Continue

Give out large sticky notes or cards at the start of a class.

Tell students that you want them to think about the session you've just led and what they feel you should:

STOP doing (what they didn't like); START doing (what they thought was missing); and CONTINUE doing (what they liked).

At the end of the session get them to hand back the sticky notes or cards with comments under stop, start or continue.

This is a really easy way of seeing what the students liked or disliked in your teaching, as well as what they were disappointed was missing.

Feedback – Tell me one thing

Hand out sticky notes at the end of your teaching session.

Tell the class to write down one thing about the session. You could vary this slightly, but make sure the question is very *open* to interpretation.

Once they have done this, they can leave the sticky notes on the wall as they leave the room.

This very open question allows the learners to tell you whatever is uppermost in their mind about your teaching session without leading them in any way towards what you expect them to say.

It can give interesting feedback regarding their perceptions of the session.

Feedback – If the session was an animal...

Tell the class to write down on a piece of paper or (large) sticky note the answer to:

"If this teaching session was an animal, what animal would it be? Then write why you picked that animal."

Once they have done this, they can leave the answers at the front of the room.

The idea of picking an animal allows the learners to tell you whatever is uppermost in their mind about your teaching session, with the "animal" acting as *permission* to give their views... as they are writing about the animal rather than just their opinions.

It can give interesting feedback regarding their perceptions of the session.

Feedback – Focus

In advance of the session, pick one aspect of your teaching, or of that particular lesson's plan, that you would like feedback on.

It may be an exercise you haven't tried before, or an aspect of your delivery you think needs improving.

Give everyone sticky notes or cards and ask 2 or 3 specific questions on *just* that very particular thing you need feedback on.

This focusses the feedback beyond the generic "it was fine" to focus on specific questions about a specific aspect of the session or your delivery and can give detailed feedback on that to help your future improvement.

Information Sources – CRAAP test house

This is related to evaluating sources of information using the CRA(A)P test (search for online examples of it!)

Split the class into small groups and give each group a couple of copies of a source of information (such as an article or book chapter), the outline of a house drawn of a large sheet of paper (flipchart paper is good), and a copy of the CRAAP test each. They will also need scissors, pens suitable for writing on flipchart paper, and glue.

Ask them to quickly scan through the "source" and work as a group to identify evidence in it against each of the CRAAP criteria. Sometimes it helps if you prompt the team to split the questions between them (so one person looks at "C" for currency another at "A", etc.)

They then cut out examples & stick them to the house (C=walls, R=downstairs windows, A=door, A=roof, P=upstairs windows). Then summarise their evidence with a sentence against each.

Ask them to share their findings with the whole class.

You can use any set of questions for assessing sources of information that you want to. Whatever you use, it can help students see the tool (like CRAAP) as a starting point, or set of interesting questions to ask about quality, rather than a check list to work through.

Information Sources - Cut & Paste

This asks your learners to physically re-arrange text from a source of information in order to practice evaluating information sources.

Give each group a large piece of paper split into sections:

- Main purpose of the article
- Key question the author is addressing
- Facts or data used
- Main conclusions
- Key concepts or theories used
- Underlying assumptions
- How it could apply to your work.

Ask them (in groups) to cut out words & phrases from an article or book chapter to sum up the above elements. They should stick these in the appropriate section.

The cutting and pasting activity can help to demystify the text and make it an accessible object for them.

They can then write a short amount of text against each point showing why they choose to cut and paste those word and phrases, in effect, answering the questions set by each section.

At the end they should sum up their collage to the whole group.

Information Sources – Found Poem

Another way of interacting with information sources in a way that makes them more accessible is to re-arrange the words within them in order to form something new.

In this exercise, give your learners copies of an article or book chapter. This could be individually, or in small groups and the article could be online, or in physical format (scissors are required for this!).

If doing the exercise in groups, these should be 2 or 3 people in each group, no more, or they will struggle to complete it.

Ask them to scan through the material and cut and paste elements to create a poem that sums up the content.

This activity forces them to quickly decide the key messages contained in the content and pull out small phrases that are key to these messages.

It develops skills in quickly reading and summing up material, as well as reducing the barrier to interacting with material that can often be scary and inaccessible to students.

It can help to limit them to a certain number of lines in their finished poem (how many depends on how much time is available).

When finished, they should name their poem (which makes them reflects on the content's meaning again) and share it with their classmates.

Information Sources – Identify some characteristics.

Sometimes students see all information as equal, especially when it appears online or out of context. Give them time to look at information sources and reflect.

Give each group an example of a type of source of information (e.g. peer reviewed journal article; trade journal; newspaper; encyclopaedia article; etc.), either originals or photocopies.

Ask students to note down some characteristics of their source. For example, "lots of references", or "short and easy to read".

Get each group to report back the characteristics and lead a discussion on what this might mean in terms of usefulness.

Information Sources – A quality investigation

First of all, find some news stories, either from the TV, newspaper or internet news source reporting on a piece of recent research that has appeared at a conference or in a journal article.

Preferably use a different one for each group in a classroom, though this isn't vital.

Split class into small groups of 2 or 3 students and give each group an example of a recent "research" news story.

Ask students to look at the news story and collect clues about the original research. They should then investigate the story using quality resources to find the real research behind the story.

Get each group to decide whether the news story accurately reflects the research or not.

This can make a good "flipped learning" exercise to do. Set the exercise a week or two before you see the students for the actual face to face session.

This can then be dedicated to reflection on the exercise and drawing out from your learners what they have learnt about the way news reports (or mis-reports) research, how they found using library resources to search for the original sources, and what these lessons may mean for how they use information in future.

Information Sources – Top sources

Give each class a set of blank cards. If you wish, you could print them yourself to look like Top Trump™ cards, but lacking text and images.

Give them a list of criteria for assessing information sources (such as CRAAP).

Ask them to work individually to think of as many different sources of information as they can and make up a "top resources" card for it (along with scores).

Then in small groups, they should share their cards and justify why they scored them the way they have.

This allows them to discuss and reflect upon the relative values of a range of information sources.

Information Sources - Jigsaws

This can help people visualise how to complete a reference.

Prepare full references on card or laminated paper, cut down into their component parts.

Split the class into small groups.

Give each group at least one example of each reference (in its component parts) for a book; journal article; website; or any other source of material you wish to cover.

Ask them to put together each reference in the correct order. You may wish to give them copies of any referencing handbook you use to make it easier.

Once they have completed one reference, they can take the components for another reference (leaving their completed references intact).

Carry on until each group has several references laid out on their tables.

Give a (small) prize for either the first team to finish, or each team to get their answers completely correct.

You can vary this by offering levels of difficulty (books = easy, conference papers = hard!), either to stretch some groups, or to allow them to gain points depending on difficulty.

When you stop the activity, ask all the groups to look at the list of references in front of them and see if they can name any of the "rules" for this referencing style.

At the end, it can be interesting to give them another reference to build (without a referencing handbook!) that they have not yet done. Most groups will be able to use the basic rules they have worked out themselves to build this new reference type.

Search – Boolean mix and match

This helps reinforce the meaning of Boolean operators in a fun, game type environment.

Prepare three sets of cards for each group. One set of cards containing the words AND, OR, NOT. The second set containing a description of the effect of these words when combining terms in a search. The third set containing a pictorial representation (a Venn diagram) of the effect of each operator.

Split the class into small groups.

Give each group the three sets of cards.

Ask them to match each Boolean operator with the correct Venn diagram and description of its effect

Give a (small) prize for the first team to finish correctly.

Search – Building a literature review

Based on "thinking with your hands" and using a model to aid reflection. It can be a risky approach, so either use as part of a wider model making workshop, or carefully "ease them in" to the idea.

Make sure everyone can reach a selection of building blocks such as Lego® to build a small model by themselves.

Ask the learners to build a model that shows the current state of their literature review.

Only give them a small amount of time to construct the model, vary this depending on how much time they seem to need! It is important that they start building quickly rather than thinking about it beforehand.

When the models are made, ask them to explain their models to the whole class. If the class is too large for this, split into small subgroups.

Common warm-ups to build up to this may be to build a model of an animal (then add bricks to show how they feel about the exercise); or build a tower as high as they can within a short time limit.

This type of exercise can be used anytime where you want a "safe" space to reflect on existing knowledge or experiences.

Many different alternative modelling materials can be used, including children's modelling clay.

For more information on this sort of approach, it might be worth looking up "Lego® Serious Play".

Search – Good and bad

Prepare handouts of a research question and a "weak" search that might be used to answer it.

Prepare a second, stronger, search to answer the same question on another handout.

Give out the "weak" search and ask your class to discuss in pairs how they might improve it. (Note – in a large class it might be easier to just show it on a screen at the front.)

Ask for suggestions on how to improve the search and discuss each suggestion.

Give out the second copy at the end to pull the discussion together.

If you have time, carry out the "weak" search at the front and show the first few results, then use their tips for improving the search – hopefully they will see the difference they make!

Search – Hang your search up

Do this after teaching the basic concepts of constructing a search strategy.

Split the class into groups and give out string, some mini-pegs and blank cards to each group. Ask them to split a research question into different topics or concepts.

Tell them to write each topic onto a piece of card. Then write other keyword or terms that could be used on their own piece of card.

Each group should then peg the keywords onto the line, grouping terms that describe the same concept together.

Ask each group to explain to the class why they picked those keywords and what boolean term would link those words pegged close together (OR) and those words in separate groups (AND).

Search – Make a Recipe

Prepare a card for each group suitable to write a recipe on – Ingredients; Method; Time; Expertise required.

When discussing techniques for effective searching, split the class into groups and ask them to come up with their own group "recipe" for an effective search. Ask them to pick a topic, or give out pre-prepared topics – one for each group.

The groups should list the "ingredients" of an effective search first, then how they combine them into a recipe that gives good results. Each group can then feedback their recipe to the whole class.

Allow plenty of time for discussion of the recipes afterwards, so the class give the main feedback to improve the recipes, with your guidance.

Search – Mind mapping

Mind maps can be an effective way of conceptualising the first stage of a search strategy. It can help to turn an assignment title into a set of research questions and concepts which could be used as initial search terms.

If your learners haven't used mind maps before, a good exercise can be to create them in groups, or as a whole class (one person at a time contributing until they run out of steam).

Give them examples of completed ones to help, then ask them to turn assignment titles into a mind map, particularly looking at the concepts they would be interested in writing about, pulling out possible search terms from them.

There are lots of free mind mapping software packages available or use (large) paper and coloured pens.

Search - What animal are you?

This is adapted from Borg, M. Stretton, E. (2009) My students and other animals. Or a vulture, an orb weaver spider, a giant panda and 900 undergraduate business students..." *Journal of Information Literacy.* 3(1), pp. 19-30.

Bring a copy per member of class of a list of animals that represent different information seeing behaviours:

Magpies are easily distracted by the new and the eye catching, ignoring other relevant material. **Cuckoos** expect others to do all the work for them. **Vultures** are scavengers, not hunters, relying on scraps of information they find lying around. **Giant anteaters** use several sources of information, but do not spend long with each source. **Ostriches** avoid looking for information, especially if it might challenge what they already know. **Squirrels** rely on information which they have previously found and stored away. **Giant pandas** rely too much on a single source of information, even if other sources are available. **Orb weaver spiders** rely exclusively on the web!

Split the class into pairs and ask them to discuss for 2 or 3 minutes a situation in which they had searched for information.

Give each member of the class a copy of the "animal typologies". They have 2 minutes to decide what animal their information seeking behaviour matches the closest.

Discuss the strengths & weaknesses of each behaviour type. This should lead into advice & discussion on how existing behaviours can be modified to make the information seeking more successful.

Search – Follow the clues

Prepare examples of a range of sources and printouts of search results.

Individually or in small groups, get them to look at one example at a time and highlight clues they might be able to follow to get some more relevant information (such as subject headings, reference lists, etc.). This could also be done to look for clues as to the quality of an information source (such as author affiliation, peer review dates, etc.).

They should then share them with the class and compile a class list of the type of "clues" they could look for and follow next time they carried out a search.

This works well if you can bring a wide range of examples for them to examine.

Warm ups – Hidden questions

If you have time to get into a classroom before the students, this is a lovely way of planting questions.

It makes the session seem more interactive, even when you need to do a lot of talking to them, as well as enabling the order / structure of the session to change each time you deliver the session.

Simply plant a set of questions in envelopes around the room on, or under, the learners' seats. Prompt them to look for these at the start of the session, which will then set up an expectation that they will be active participants in the session (and can't passively sit back and let things wash over them!).

Warm ups - Music

I've put this as a warm up, but I also use it when I want to signify a change at other times during a session.

Play music when people come into the room for a start of a session, preferably to suit the lesson coming up (so don't play something too up tempo if you want them to be calm… or depressing & slow if you want them to be full of energy!).

When you are ready to start, turn the music down, then off. The change in background noise will often prompt people to go quiet without further action on your part.

It works the same to signify the end of group work during a session, especially if you can find a music track of the correct length to suit!

Warm ups – Pass the parcel

I've used this as a fun way to structure a session which was mainly group work, with each layer giving the group their instructions. As a warm up though, it is great way to give people "permission to play" at the start.

Create a parcel with alternating layers of coloured paper. In each layer is a small prize (such as sweets) and a question. Play some music, and the learners must pass the parcel between themselves until the music stops. Then they reveal a question and a prize. The questions can either be something for them to answer, or to read out for someone else to answer.

Easily scaled up to a lecture theatre, as you can have several parcels at the same time.

Warm ups – Quick Question

A non-threatening way of collecting information about your learners and what they need from your session.

It doesn't take long, but the more learners, the longer it will take you to look through them.

If in small groups, give a piece of card to each group, if in a lecture theatre, one to each row. Ask them to write down the main thing they'd like to learn from the session, then pass in to the next person in the row / group. They should do the same, or tick anything already written down. When it has worked its way through the group / to the end of the row, collect the card.

Flick through them and make sure you cover anything with several ticks!

Further Reading

Accardi, M. T., & Vukovic, J. (2013). *Feminist pedagogy for library instruction.* Sacramento, California: Library Juice Press.

A lovely book that combines theory and practical examples that can help you to develop a feminist pedagogy in your own teaching.

Bates, B. (2016). *Learning theories simplified and how to apply them to teaching.* London: SAGE.

Ever talked to an academic and been baffled by talk of 'behaviourism', 'constructivism', or other learning theory type stuff? This brilliant book sums up all the –isms you're likely to come across in a really accessible way. The best crib sheet I've ever come across for learning and pedagogical theories.

Blanchett, H., Powis, C., & Webb, J. (2012). *A guide to teaching information literacy: 101 practical tips*. London: Facet.

Written by three experienced librarians, this is a good collection of practical teaching tips directly aimed at librarians who teach.

Eastwood, L., Coates, J., Dixon, L., Harvey, J., Ormondroyd, C., Williamson, S. (2009). *A toolkit for creative teaching in post-compulsory education.* Maidenhead: Open University Press.

Full of creative ideas for teaching anyone in 16+ education, many of these can apply to library teaching. One to dip into and get a wide range of creative ideas to apply to your own teaching.

Gröppel-Wegener, A. (2016). *Writing essays by pictures: A workbook.* Huddersfield: Innovative Libraries.

This is a practical workbook aimed at undergraduates, but just as suitable for anyone 16+ who needs to write an essay. It takes you through a series of practical exercises that build the skills needed for essay writing. There are lots of ideas here that could be taken and used for teaching information and academic skills separately to the whole workbook!

Petty, G., & Petty, G. (2014). Teaching today: A practical guide (Fifth ed.). Oxford: Oxford University Press.

This is often a standard text book for trainee teachers. It is very practical in style and full of tips that can be easily applied in library settings.

Pagowsky, N., & McElroy, K. (2016). *Critical library pedagogy*. Chicago: Association of College and Research Libraries.

There are two volumes of this, and it's quite expensive to buy. If you can persuade your library to buy it – great. If it's just for you, many of the contributors have put their chapters online in institutional repositories, so you can dip into it even if you can't afford the 'full' version. If you've heard of critical library pedagogy but not sure what it means or how to apply it to your own practice, this is the place to go!

Secker, J., & Coonan, E. (2013). *Rethinking information literacy: A practical framework for supporting learning.* London: Facet Publishing.

Recommended as a way of refreshing how you think of information literacy and the teaching of it, to help reflect on what and how you teach. Jane and Emma developed the ANCIL framework (A New Curriculum for Information Literacy) together.

Feedback please!

This book is the second edition, tweaked based upon feedback from the first! People liked the small, compact nature (except when trying to shelve in a library!) of the book and the cheap price! Some asked for it to be longer, and said that although it was nice that lots of the tips and ideas were on one page, they could just as well be spread over two when it was necessary to make things clearer.

So this version has more of the ideas spread over two pages, as well as extra tips and ideas, which together extended it by about 50% compared to the first edition.

If you'd like to suggest a tip for inclusion in a future edition, please send it to me for consideration. (Approx. 100 words)

andywalsh@innovativelibraries.org.uk

Selected other books from Innovative Libraries Press:

The librarians' book on teaching through games and play is aimed mainly at staff in libraries, especially those who teach information skills, this book contains many examples of games and playful interactions to help turn the information literacy classroom into a more playful space.

Standard "list price" £20

ISBN 978-1-911500-07-0

"Learning through metaphor: An introduction to metaphors in information literacy" is a short book on the use of metaphor in library teaching.

Elizabeth Brown has written a small, practical, and affordable introduction for anyone interested in using metaphor in their library teaching

This book is due out in the last quarter of 2018.

Expected standard "list price" £9.95 (TBC)

Print ISBN: 978-1911500094

"Writing Essays By Pictures" uses visual analogies to explain all the bits that go into researching and writing at degree level, particularly those steps that often remain hidden to students at their first try.

Writing Essays by Pictures explains the basics of academic research to the beginner - and to people who have always wished for a way to make these things visual... and fun!

It is a practical workbook that can be used by students, as well as a source of inspiration for teaching information and academic skills to students.

Standard "list price" £15

Print ISBN: 978-0957665224

Lightning Source UK Ltd.
Milton Keynes UK
UKHW02f2237310818
328138UK00011B/98